The
Adventures
of
Egbert
the
Easter Egg

Also by Richard Armour
with pictures by Paul Galdone
THE YEAR SANTA WENT MODERN

McGraw-Hill Book Company   *New York · Toronto · London*

THE ADVENTURES OF
Egbert
THE EASTER EGG

by
Richard Armour

Paul Galdone
drew
the pictures

Egbert

the egg looked like other eggs:

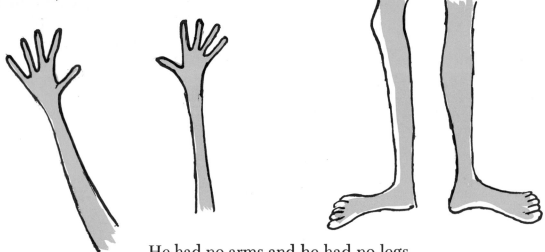

He had no arms and he had no legs

And he had no face.

All he had, for skin,
Was a very thin shell, to keep insides in.

And so if you looked where he lay with dozens
Of just-alike eggs, Egbert's brothers and cousins,
Without any name on,
Not even an "E,"
How in the world would you know which was he?

Try putting yourself in his place—or his shell—
Wouldn't *you* be unhappy if no one could tell?

One day, though (this state of affairs couldn't last),
Things started to happen to Egbert—and fast.
It was just before Easter when suddenly he
Heard voices of children all shouting with glee:
"We're having an Easter egg hunt! Hooray!"
"We'll color the eggs, Mother says, today!"
"I'm painting mine yellow,"
"I'm painting mine green."
"I'm painting mine purple,
With pink in between."

Then Egbert was suddenly given a hoist
And plopped into water that made him all moist.
"Delightful," thought Egbert. "Delightfully cool." . . .
Then it grew much too warm. "This is no swimming pool!"
It bubbled and boiled and the eggs took a belting,
Till one of them cried, "Help! I think I am melting."
Said another, more wise, "You're not melting, my lad,
But a hotter hot bath I never have had."
And Egbert, who'd been a bit sloshy inside,
And was fearful of cracking,
Could feel, with some pride,
He was growing hard boiled, and so sturdy, in fact,
He had nothing to fear if ever he cracked.
"My insides will stay
Inside me," he thought,
"If somebody throws me
And I am not caught."

Soon out of the water and ranged in a row
Were Egbert and others, all ready to go.

Then paint started flowing, for each boy and girl
Was dipping
And daubing
With flourish and swirl.
Some painted straight stripes,
While some painted circles,

Still others made lines
That had crookedy quirkles.
The boys painted broadly,
The girls were more dainty,
And some missed the eggs
And themselves were all painty.

What happened to Egbert?
What happened was plenty.
He didn't get circles
Or stripes, ten or twenty.
But thanks to the owner whose egg Egbert was,
He got something better than any, because
The boy, a small fellow the others called Frank,
Having noticed that Egbert was perfectly blank,
Quite thoughtfully painted,
And in the right place,
What Egbert had needed and longed for—

A FACE!

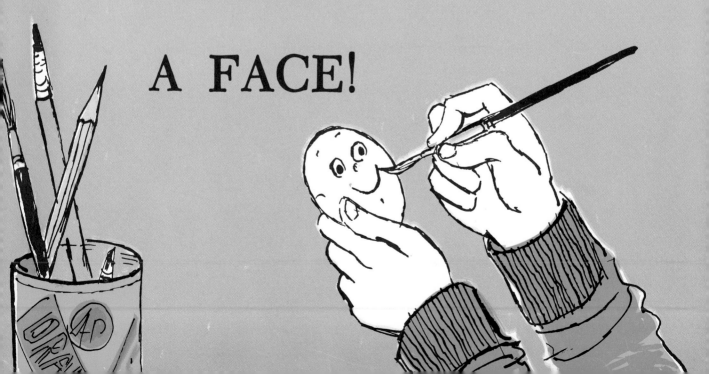

Let other eggs boast of their pretty designs,
Their straight and their wavy and zig-zaggy lines.
Egbert alone
Had two eyes, round and wide,
And a couple of ears,
One ear to a side,
And a dot of a nose and a happy-smile mouth
And a small, dimpled chin
Underneath, to the south.

Oh, Egbert was proud of his face as could be,
Since no other egg had a face—only he.
Though his eyes weren't quite even,
And likewise his ears,
Egbert thought to himself,

"I've a *face* now. Three cheers!
I'm sure I'll be placed in a place up in front
And be the first found in the Easter egg hunt.
With a face such as this, I most certainly know
That I'll be the big smash
(No, the hit)
Of the show."

Came the day of the hunt.
The parents that morning
Without any hint
And without any warning
Hid Easter eggs easterly,
Westerly, northerly,
In places up neartherly,
Also out fartherly.

They put them below things
And also behind things,
Where no one, you'd think,
Would be looking to find things:
In boxes, in barrels, in trees, and in hedges,
In holes
Dug by moles
And on out-of-sight ledges.
They hid the eggs lowly,
They hid the eggs highly,
They hid the eggs ever so shrewdly
And slyly,
Then said, when they'd finished, with eggs in the flowers
And eggs behind bricks: "They'll be busy for hours."

But when, at a signal, the children came hopping
And leaping and laughing, to seek without stopping,
They made a beeline for each egg where it lay
(For parents aren't very good hiders-away).
And cries of "I've found one!"
"I've found one!" "I've found one!"
Soon filled all the garden
And echoed around one.
Ten minutes or less—
Maybe five—and they'd got
All the eggs that were hidden.

That is, so they thought.

THEY HADN'T FOUND EGBERT.
And what, I insist,
Hurt Egbert still more was—
He hadn't been missed!
For Frank, who'd have known
And would gladly have told,
Was at home, as happened,
In bed with a cold.

Yes, Frank, who had painted on Egbert's white space,
Would have asked, were he there,
"Where's the egg with a face?"
But Frank was at home with a cough and a sniffle,
And to anyone else one more egg was but piffle.

20

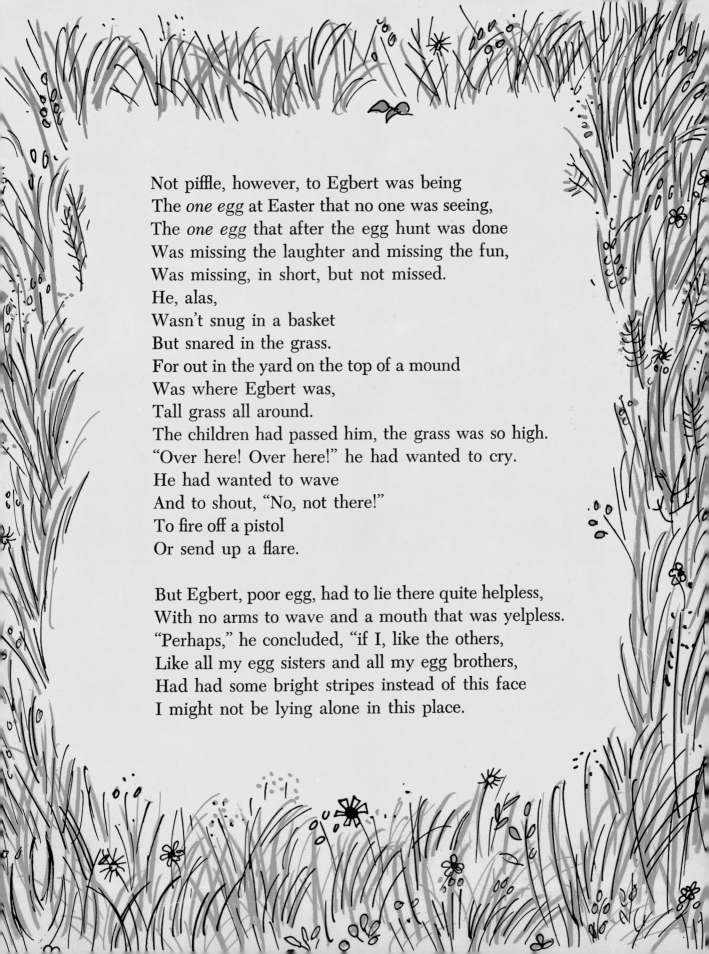

Not piffle, however, to Egbert was being
The *one egg* at Easter that no one was seeing,
The *one egg* that after the egg hunt was done
Was missing the laughter and missing the fun,
Was missing, in short, but not missed.
He, alas,
Wasn't snug in a basket
But snared in the grass.
For out in the yard on the top of a mound
Was where Egbert was,
Tall grass all around.
The children had passed him, the grass was so high.
"Over here! Over here!" he had wanted to cry.
He had wanted to wave
And to shout, "No, not there!"
To fire off a pistol
Or send up a flare.

But Egbert, poor egg, had to lie there quite helpless,
With no arms to wave and a mouth that was yelpless.
"Perhaps," he concluded, "if I, like the others,
Like all my egg sisters and all my egg brothers,
Had had some bright stripes instead of this face
I might not be lying alone in this place.

Or if I'd had colorful spots, then I might
Have been spotted and not
Be alone here all night."

All night he was there, it was woefully true,
A night that was chilly and rainy too.
Poor Egbert, his face facing up at the sky,
Saw the heavy black rain clouds go scuttering by,
And he felt things come crawling
From holes in the ground
That brushed him
And nudged him
And slithered around.
It might be a snake
Or a snail
Or a worm
Or something still worse
With a horrible squirm.

But Egbert, face up, couldn't see if he tried
What burrowed beneath him or brushed on his side.
Indeed, were he able, he wouldn't have peered,
For Egbert, alone in the darkness,
Was skeered.

A bird with great beak and with talons like metal
Once swooped, about midnight, and started to settle
Right smack upon Egbert, then noting his face
Said, "Oops, it appears that I've got the wrong place.
I have to be going, to get to my garden."
Then it left with a flap and "I beg, sir, your pardon."

Egbert suffered intensely from cold and from fear,
And the long, lonely night seemed a month or a year,

But morning arrived, as it has a way
Of doing, and it was EASTER DAY.
And the sky was bright and the sun was warm
And Egbert no longer felt any alarm
When he heard a strange sound or he felt a new nudge.
In fact once he muttered quite bravely, "Oh, fudge!"

Then a strange thing happened.

Thanks to the rain
That had fallen all night
And had formed a drain—
A river or rivulet ever more wide
That flowed around Egbert on either side—

With a twist and a twitch Egbert started to move
Through the grass where the drain made an egg-sized groove.
On out to the edge of the mound he hobbled
And slipped and skidded and wiggled and wobbled.
Then over the edge and down, uncontrolled,
Egbert faster and *faster* and FASTER rolled.
As Egbert gained speed, with the greatest of ease
He rolled down the mound
And around shrubs and trees.
He rolled across lawns newly mowed. What a roller!
He rolled like a bowling ball bowled by a bowler.

He rolled like a golf ball that rolls in the fairway.
He rolled like a marble that's dropped on the stairway.
Breaking every known record for eggs, I am told,
He rolled and he rolled and he rolled
And he rolled.
He rolled to the sidewalk,
He rolled to the street,
Just missing by inches all manner of feet;
The feet of gay people, of man and of maid,
Parading, today, in the Easter Parade.

And where, then, did Egbert, who spun like a top,
When his rolling was done, come at last to a stop?
Can you possibly guess? Have you any vague notion?
Did he drop down a drainpipe
And wash to the ocean?
Did he vanish forever in leaves and in trash?
Did the wheel of a car, with a terrible smash—
A passenger car or a truck with a load—
Make Egbert the egg but a spot in the road?

If these were your guesses, you couldn't be wronger.
I'll tell you what happened, not take any longer.

He stopped by the steps of a small, pleasant place,
The home of the boy who had painted his face.
And Frank, who'd stayed home from the Easter egg hunt,
Was watching the crowds from a window
In front,
And he saw there the egg with its small face upturned,
The face of poor Egbert.
How Egbert then yearned
To hear as the eggs at the egg hunt had heard,
"I've *found* one!" (To eggs, what a welcoming word!)
And better than anything else, great or grand,
To feel, warm around him, a little child's hand. . . .

Did Frank come a-running? He did, right away,
On, it happened, his happiest Easter Day.
Did he say, then, "I've found one"?
No, see the next line:

He said (Egbert loved him for this), "I've found *mine!*"